T0080630

MYSTERIES OF THE
MAYA

PATHFINDER EDITION

By Brent Goff and Kenneth Garrett

CONTENTS

CRACKING THE CODE

Who were the ancient Maya? Clues may be hidden in the mysterious writing they left behind.

light lit up a wall.

MAYA MYSTERY

David's curiosity soared as he observed drawings and **hieroglyphs,** or glyphs, on the walls. He was looking at ancient Maya writing. He was anxious to know what the glyphs said. Maybe they could help solve the mysteries of the Maya!

The **quest** to crack the Maya code, or puzzle of Maya writing, began 170 years ago, long before David was born. Back then, Maya cities were mostly the stuff of legend, and many people wondered if they really existed.

In 1839, two explorers decided to find out. They trekked through the dense, dark jungles of Central America, where they discovered pyramids wrapped in vines and glyphs carved in stone. Over time, the explorers visited the ruins of 44 Maya cities. The book they wrote about their findings made others want to know more about the Maya.

DIGGING FOR CLUES

Archaeologists began digging for answers—literally. Over time, they found buildings, ball fields, and even tombs that had been buried beneath the jungle. They dug up pottery, jewelry, and other clues to how the Maya lived long ago.

The clues told them that the Maya thrived from 250 C.E. to 900 C.E. in surprisingly large cities. The ruins at Tikal in Guatemala, for example, include 3,000 stone buildings, and as many as 90,000 people once lived there. As they explored further, archaeologists realized that the Maya had no metal tools; yet they built pyramids and temples that rose 40 meters (130 feet) high!

Archaeologists also discovered that each city was like a small country ruled by a king. Pictures of the revered monarchs were painted and carved in stone in many public places. Other kinds of art gave archaeologists clues about Maya culture. For example, some Maya art shows a rough game played with a rubber ball. How rough? Losing players faced death.

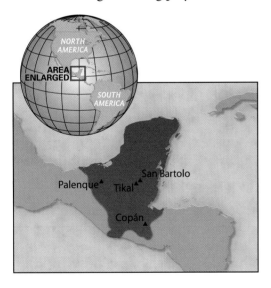

GLYPH MYSTERY

Archaeologists also found many glyphs. The Maya had carved glyphs into pyramid steps and stone sculptures and painted them on walls of buildings and on pottery.

These finds sparked the quest to **decipher** the Maya code. Epigraphers, or experts in ancient writing, studied the glyphs. Maybe the glyphs were just pictures, but what if they were a form of writing? Code breakers wondered if the Maya left a "map" of how to read the glyphs.

In the early 1800s, the world buzzed with excitement about the Rosetta Stone. Discovered in Egypt in 1799, the stone had ancient Egyptian and Greek writing on it. **Scholars** could read the Greek, so they used it to decode Egyptian hieroglyphs. Maya scholars wondered if Maya hieroglyphs had a Rosetta Stone, too.

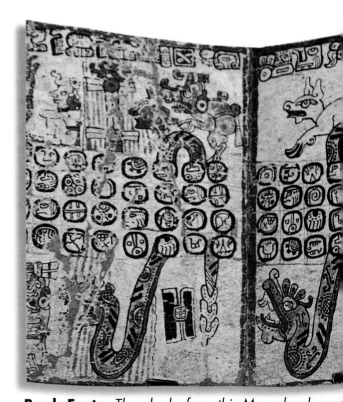

Book Facts. *The glyphs from this Maya book exp*

TIME LINE

250–900	1500s	1799
Ancient Maya civilization thrives in Central America.	The Spanish begin their conquest of Central America.	The Rosetta Stone is used as the key to understanding Egyptian hieroglyphs.

EARLY LEADS

The hunt was on! Clues led code breakers to Europe. They knew that back in the 1500s, the Spaniards had conquered parts of Central America. Maybe some of the Spanish conquistadors had taken home Maya treasures.

By the mid-1800s, code breakers had found three Maya books. Two were discovered in libraries in Germany and France, and a Spanish family had the third. Scholars now had more glyphs to study and try to decipher.

Then, in 1862, Maya code breakers got a big break, or so they hoped. One found an old book written by Spanish priest Diego de Landa, who had lived with the Maya in the 1500s. In his book, Landa matched some glyphs to letters in the Spanish alphabet. Was this the key to cracking the Maya glyphs?

TIME TRACKERS

Code breakers tried to use Landa's alphabet to read the Maya books, but they couldn't make sense of the glyphs. Still, they didn't give up.

In the 1880s, a scholar noticed a pattern of bars and dots in the glyphs and realized the Maya had a counting system. The Maya even drew a shell to stand for zero.

Maya math quickly led to another big discovery—the glyphs were full of numbers. Once scholars could read those bars and dots, they realized many numbers were dates. The Maya had a calendar!

The Maya wrote dates to record the movement of the stars and planets. That's how they kept track of time. They even used the changing position of the planet Venus to plan wars. If they could see Venus in the western sky, it could be a good time to fight!

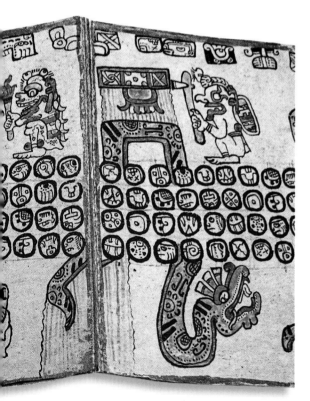

best days to plant corn and collect honey.

Kingly Carving.
To celebrate a battle victory, the Maya made this wood carving of the ruler of Tikal.

1839	**1862**	**1880s**	**1980**
Explorers discover Maya ruins.	Landa's book gives phonetic matches for some Maya glyphs.	Scholars discover Maya numbers and calendar.	David Stuart discovers that Maya words can be written in multiple ways.

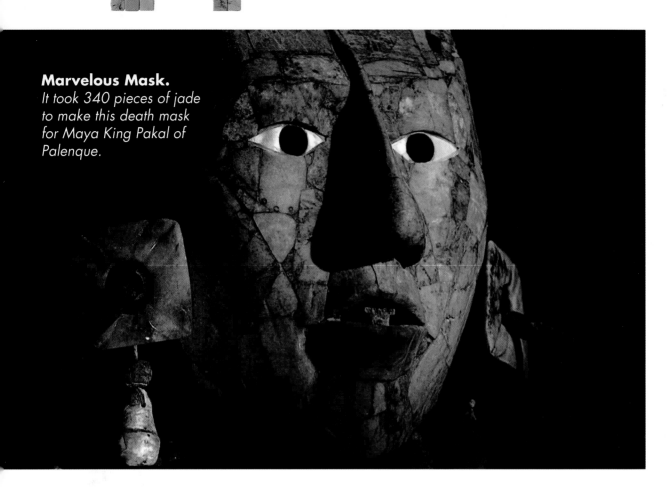

Marvelous Mask.
It took 340 pieces of jade
to make this death mask
for Maya King Pakal of
Palenque.

BREAKING THE CODE

By the 1950s, code breakers had identified 800 glyphs, but
they still couldn't read most of them. Were the meanings
lost forever?

Then code breakers slowly began seeing more
patterns in the glyphs. Some seemed to be the names
of places, while others stood for words, like "born"
or "died." These glyphs often had carvings of people
next to them. They must tell stories of Maya rulers!

Code breakers also realized many glyphs are
phonetic, or stand for sounds, not words. Landa's
"alphabet" began to make sense, and by 1980,
code breakers understood about 75 percent of
the glyphs.

Look for Labels. What was this pot used
for? There's a clue written on it. The middle
glyph on the rim stands for the word cacao,
which means "chocolate."

6

CAVE KEY

That's the year David made his hot, sweaty trip to the cave. The teen already was **intrigued** by glyphs. He stared at the cave wall and felt his excitement grow. David read a date: 741 C.E.

David looked at a nearby word. He thought it was *Pax*, the name of the 16th month in the Maya calendar. Still, it looked different. He sounded it out: *Pa-xa*. It was *Pax*, but written in a different way. David had just read a Maya glyph no code breaker had ever decoded before.

David became a Maya epigrapher, or expert on Maya glyphs. In time, his discoveries helped lead to a new way of reading them. The Maya drew different glyphs to stand for the same sounds. It's a bit like English, where the *f* and *ph* look different but sound the same.

It took decades of hard work; yet David and other epigraphers had deciphered the Maya code! Now they could learn more about the lives of the ancient Maya.

SHARING SECRETS

Meanwhile, archaeologists continue to dig up many secrets of the Maya. Still, artifacts don't tell the whole story. Luckily, the glyphs help fill in the details. Some trace the rise and fall of royal families, while others tell of leaders with names like Fire Is Born and Bird Jaguar.

Scholars once thought the Maya loved peace, but the glyphs tell a different story. Some describe bloody battles and wars waged by power-hungry Maya kings.

The glyphs also provide clues to daily life. For example, archaeologists thought Maya rulers drank chocolate. The glyphs helped prove it. One day, David read a glyph on a clay pot that said *cacao*, or "chocolate." Scientists tested a similar pot with the same glyph written on it—it still had bits of chocolate in it!

MYSTERIES REMAIN

Today, code breakers can read about 95 percent of Maya glyphs. This hasn't solved all the Maya mysteries, however. After 900 C.E., most great Maya cities emptied, but no glyphs explain what happened. Perhaps the Maya ran out of food or had too many wars.

Questions remain, yet new finds keep adding to what's known about the Maya. Not long ago, David visited Maya ruins in San Bartolo, Guatemala. He saw glyphs written between 300 B.C.E. and 200 B.C.E. painted on a wall. It was the oldest Maya writing ever found! Now he was one step closer to knowing when the Maya first learned to write.

What secrets do these new glyphs hold? No one is sure. They look different, and many can't be read yet. Code breakers have a new puzzle to solve. And so the quest continues to find the glyphs' meanings—and make sure they are never lost again.

WORDWISE

decipher: to figure out the meaning of something

hieroglyph: writing that uses shapes to stand for words or word parts

intrigue: to make somebody very interested in something

quest: a journey in search of something

scholar: a person who has studied something deeply

Where Did They Go?

By Kenneth Garrett

NATIONAL GEOGRAPHIC PHOTOGRAPHER

Big City. *Palenque was one of the Maya's greatest cities. The tower at the left is part of a large, stone palace.*

A lost world lies hidden in the rain forests of Central America. Hundreds of cities and towns stand among the trees. Once they were home to millions of Native Americans known as the Maya.

Today those cities are empty. Tree limbs and vines embrace the old buildings, and many once proud temples now stand in ruins.

What happened to the Maya? Why did they flee their beautiful cities? Archaeologists have been asking these questions for years.

So have I. As a photographer for National Geographic, I have watched as new discoveries **reveal** answers to questions about Maya civilization, which flourished between 250 C.E. to 900 C.E.

On a recent assignment, I visited the ancient Maya city of San Bartolo, where some of the earliest remains of Maya civilization are now being unearthed.

Glimpses of the Early Maya

People began building San Bartolo about 2,500 years ago. They constructed large stone pyramids, including one around 30 meters (98 feet) high. To the Maya, pyramids stood for mountains, which the Maya thought were holy because they reached toward the sky.

The city of San Bartolo contains many surprises. At the base of one pyramid is a room full of beautiful **murals** that Maya artists painted about 2,100 years ago.

When scientists found the murals only a few years ago, it was a huge discovery. Before then, archaeologists had not known that the early Maya were such skilled artists.

A **tomb** holding a king's body lies west of the pyramid. Before finding the tomb in 2005, scientists had not found any early Maya kings.

In addition, scientists found some glyphs nearby. The symbols represent some of the oldest Maya writing ever discovered and may hold clues to its development.

Clearly, San Bartolo is a treasure trove for Maya scholars, but it isn't the only Maya place.

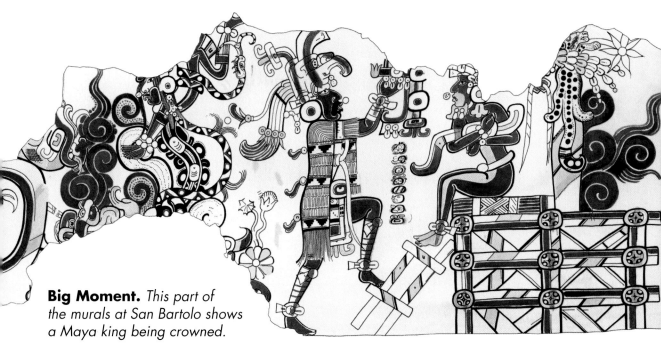

Big Moment. *This part of the murals at San Bartolo shows a Maya king being crowned.*

Cities of Stone

One of my favorite Maya places is Copán, one of the greatest Maya cities.

About 1,600 years ago, Copán was just a small town, with perhaps 3,000 residents. Then, over hundreds of years, its rulers began to build temples and pyramids, one after another.

One king would build something; then a new king would build right on top of it. As a result, the place is like a giant layer cake of Maya history.

The city of Copán grew with its buildings. In time, some 20,000 people lived there. Of course, Copán was small compared to Tikal.

Roughly 1,300 years ago, as many as 90,000 people lived in Tikal. They worked and lived among 3,000 major buildings, including plazas, palaces, and pyramids. Nestled deep in the Guatemalan rain forest, Tikal is one of the most beautiful places I've ever seen.

Parts of Copán and Tikal still stand today. They're impressive. They're even more impressive when you know that the Maya did not use wheels to move stones, and they had no horses to pull heavy loads. They did all this work themselves.

Maya Life

Who lived in and near these great cities? Most Maya were ordinary people living in wooden houses around the cities' edges.

There they raised corn, which was their main food. Men grew the corn, and women ground it into flour to make flat cakes called tortillas.

Some people had special skills. They were artists, potters, weavers, writers, and more. One of the Maya people's most remarkable skills was their ability to predict changes in the sky. They charted the paths of the moon, planets, and stars. Astronomers and other such skilled workers likely lived in small stone houses.

Then there were the rulers. Maya kings and nobles wanted people to think of them as gods, so they lived in style. I once took photos of a Maya **palace** in the ancient city of Palenque.

The palace was a huge, stone building, with many rooms and fine carvings. Clearly, this home belonged to someone important!

By 1,200 years ago, the Maya had been around for hundreds of years, and it seemed like life would never change. Then it did.

Bird Man. *People used this clay vessel to burn incense. The figure is a Maya warrior wearing an eagle headdress.*

Into the Air? *Modern Maya try flying a traditional kite. Some kites are 8 meters (25 feet) across.*

Hard Times

Change came quickly to the Maya world. The great cities of the rain forest stopped growing, and people gave up making great buildings. Then they moved away, and soon, whole cities lay empty.

What happened? No one knows. One theory is that constant warfare weakened the great cities. Another is that Maya farming destroyed the land. **Drought** probably also hurt the Maya. Without rain, they couldn't grow the food they needed to sustain their large population.

The Maya story doesn't end there, however. Maya people didn't just disappear. North of the rain forests, new cities arose and thrived for several hundred years.

Then came the Spanish, who conquered Central America about 500 years ago. That meant more changes for the Maya. Many Maya, for example, began speaking Spanish.

Great Maya Moments

You see, the Maya did not really "go" anywhere. The ancestors of the ancient Maya live on today. They speak Mayan languages and practice many old customs. On one visit, I was lucky enough to witness one.

People flew huge, round kites as the Maya did in the old days. The kites stood for messages to family members who had died. Everyone tried to fly the kites as high as they could, so their messages would reach the heavens.

Photographing those kites was a great moment. It showed me that the Maya culture lives on. Actually, taking photos of the Maya world is full of great moments. I can't wait for the next one!

Wordwise

drought: lack of rain

mural: a large wall painting

palace: the home of a king or other ruler

reveal: to make known

tomb: a building where a dead body is kept

MANY MYSTERIES

Be a code breaker. Find the answers to these questions about the Maya.

1 Why is David Stuart's work so important?

2 Look at the time line. What event took place in the 1500s? How does this event help you understand Maya history?

3 How does Kenneth Garrett explain where the Maya went?

4 How does Maya civilization compare with the civilization of ancient Egypt?

5 How have David Stuart and Kenneth Garrett helped to save a piece of the world?